desultory sonnets

desultory sonnets

ted jean

Desultory Sonnets
Copyright © 2016 Ted Jean
Winner, 2016 Turtle Island Poetry Award

Turtle Island Quarterly sponsors the annual Turtle Island Poetry Award. Awards are chosen by the editors. More information available at http://fourdirectionpoetry.wixsite.com/turtleisland

Cover image by Ted Jean

First Flowstone Press Edition, November 2016
ISBN-13 978-1-945824-02-9

This little book is for Amy Lee,
who appears in several of its poems.
All of them, really.

Table of Contents

	Introduction, by Jared Smith	vii
I	Sonnet recited in one long breath	3
II	Hwy 38 on the Umpqua near Rainrock	4
III	Regarding Wife	5
IV	cover	6
V	warts across the flank of infinity	7
VI	rehearsal	8
VII	mendicant	9
VIII	Gull Sutra	10
IX	"… like a green girl, unsifted in such perilous circumstances"	11
X	Unified Field Theory	12
XI	Robinson Creek	13
XII	minor enigma	14
XIII	Exercise no. 38	15
XIV	Two Rivers	16
XV	Callus	17
XVI	Deep Weed Theory	18
XVII	weeds	19
XVIII	*amaranthus viridis*	20
XIX	Hwy 99 North of Aurora	21
XX	Alcoholic	22
XXI	Bliss Road, west Benton County	23
XXII	Seeing Things	24
XXIII	unchosen	25
XXIV	regarding wife	26

Introduction

By Jared Smith

How is it possible for a sonnet—that precise, tired, old, formulaic European form of poetry—to be "desultory," or as that word implies unplanned and haphazard? Well, it takes a master craftsman of enormous creative talent and vision to accomplish the writing of one. Ted Jean has done so, not once but with a whole sequence of them. These are sonnets alright, but not of the egg-carton form we learned of in school. They are sonnets of organic form that matches the wild uncultivated landscape from which they come. Like the wild grasses and sedges and the edges of town of which they speak, they have a form which fits the free and meditative moments that line the peripheries of our lives, shaped by the winds that blow over them.

These are *varied* sonnets—a whole sumptuous sequence of shifting emotional preludes noted down by a poet who is a painter of vivid imagery that echoes from one poem to another, thereby extending the experience. No two sonnets have quite the same shape or tone as any other, or use the same forms in the same way, though they echo in their desultory fashion the old formulas from which they take their name. There are modified Petrarchan sonnets and modified Shakespearean ones, and many other subsets and take-offs from what other master poets have done, and they pay strong homage to those past writers although the forms of these sonnets are wider and more open to the fresh air and night sky than what those earlier writers have done. There are octaves and sestets in many of them, and there are triple quatrains ended by couplets. There are hints of iambic strings and slant rhyme and alliteration, and other echoes of tradition. But they have twigs hanging off those forms, branches breaking off, limbs waving wildly. Their forms are organic, rather than formulaic, and in that their perfection lies. Virtually all of them, but not quite, consist of the traditional 14 lines, but they are not in pentameter, none of them are—breaking shape and meter, and stripping down to the size befitting the moment; in one particular sonnet to a form that is more reminiscent of Richard Kostelanetz and the avante garde than of the Romantics. Seldom have I seen such variety and such mastery of structure and vision within a single collection—and certainly within one sequence.

That brings us to another and perhaps even more subtle area of questioning. At first reading, one might wonder why these poems, these *desultory* sonnets, can be deemed a sequence that is worthy of standing as a fully formed chapbook. Can a sequence be unplanned and haphazard, even as the structure of the poems themselves has proven to be? The tone and mood of the poems *feel* sequential, but in terms of linear narrative, there is none. Nor is there a linear growth of discovery. But it works. What does structurally link these sonnets into one very powerful and lovely sequence is much more ethereal and meaningful. It is the image of a lovely young woman looking out over a landscape and time that encompasses the roads and gardens and mountains of our known world, and of her gazing through that world into more distant and unknowable worlds and visions. As the poet says when he first introduces her as Regarding Wife in sonnet III, there is no way of knowing what is going on in her mind or what she is seeing—but through her intensity of peace it is clear that it is meaningful, and as the poet says it "rolls out over the void on a unique arc." In sonnet IV, he speaks of "your scoriated heart, the often broken creek" that cannot often be mended. In sonnet V, this vision of melding between our lives, or the woman's life, and that of the larger world is expanded to include a vision where "between the leaf being bright,/ and light again/ lies an eternity of darkness." Beyond that light and dark eternity, in sonnet XVII, he notes that regardless, all things are "ugly in any case,/ unless, as with many things, you sit and watch awhile."

This is important, and once discovered it provides a hypnotic and powerful structure for the whole sequence. This understated and organic vision of a woman looking off into time and distance and trying to organize that which is beyond her with a force that we are unable to see or fathom is present throughout the entire sequence, once it has been identified, and it is haunting. It is the organizing power of thought and emotion against the universe. Does this patient and intense watching and whatever goes on inside of ourselves because of it in fact change or give form to anything? We must believe it does, if we are to believe in structure or music or poetry or love. Do we see it separately from the art it reflects in…perhaps, or perhaps not. But it drives the lives of those who are artists, poets, and lovers… and it is beyond our flesh and what we leave behind. "Ditch the body, what remains?/a wave of transport proceeding from now to no particular where." This then is a wave of transport, from here into that which is greater, and it pulls us along. Sonnet XXIV is the final sonnet in the sequence, and it is only the second time we "see" the woman or guess at what has become of her—for she is there only in memory or thought. Of "Precautions against her being/ gone, there is no record."

This is a deeply moving, masterfully crafted collection. It will transport you into a higher state of awareness of life and what is about us.

desultory sonnets

I

Sonnet recited in one long breath

Who? for Chrissake, would chuck
a big quince branch
pregnant with incipient bloom
over the fence onto my frosty lawn
except as a kind of anonymous gift
that if undiscovered a week
would be withered and wasted
and now stands
instead quite fortuitously
blazing
coral and white and bloody red
in a big blue vase
on the mahogany piano
by the window green with rain

II

Hwy 38 along the Umpqua near Rainrock

High crow and low crow
ply the light above the river,
rising and falling against the neon backdrop alder.

One seems the shadow of the other,
disjunct in their dithering
as a fish with its refraction on a riffled pond.

Are they husband and wife crow?
Where do they go?
Some farcical mission, doubtless,
as they are, after all, crows.

We are driving upriver the opposite way,
Amy staring off into the spruce shadow
and sunlight strobe, possibly deep in thought.
Or not. We will never know.

III

Regarding wife

She is no warmer than merely mammal.
Her breath ticks like the twitter of insects
sewn thickly on the grassier planets.
Her scent the incense of corporality,
no holier than one horse or another.
Her bare legs the complex but common
function of oil and muscle and motion;
certainly somewhere there are better.
Her long black hair is the hair of virtually
all Chinese girls; her closed eyes precisely
the color you might guess; her lightly
burnished white gold skin could be
assigned, I suppose, to simply yellow.

She moves against me, and the world
rolls out over the void on a unique arc

IV

cover

you have been injured. again.
rehearse the old algorithm, about
breathing, bleeding less, finding cover.

where is the creek?
down the scree, scramble;
skid through the astringent brush.

bleed into the creek,
drink more of its gin by a factor of four;
bury your hobbled ankles in its gravel.

find a spot on a rock to receive the sun.
if the current suggests laughter, accept.
accept the circling red refracted crawdads.

your scoriated heart, the often broken
creek … they probably cannot be stopped.

V

Warts across the flank of infinity

The hawking eorl
hankered by his unblindered bird
to gauge the world
beyond his brute legs, and
gazing, he got, he thought,
the celestial knot of it.

Stephen argues halt
singular questions, his palsied palms
flashing cards crossed with
inelegant ciphers, perhaps
persuasive, as his parting wife
collapses into a black hole.

Between the leaf being bright,
and light again,
    lies an eternity of darkness.

VI

Rehearsal

Ben bought Plot No. 8
in the Old Section
of the Taft Pioneer Cemetery
with a crumpled check left over
in the glove box of his Ford pickup

he walked the beach two hours,
bought a cheap sleeping bag
at the K Mart across from the Indian casino,
had three Scotches
at the Blue Cedar Bar on C Street

and slept like the dead
in the weeds on Plot No. 8
while a restless westerly blew
over him all that dreamless night

VII

mendicant

four o'clock coffee:
first baking from the Sellwood Safeway

    risen early with no real purpose,
    no plane to catch, a habit shaped
    equally of anxiety and autonomy

enter gull:
flare to pavement, pas de chat, perfunctory poop

    behind the wheel of his pickup,
    the most personal private space
    on the face of the rearview world

stare-down:
beggar bird has the upper hand, and knows it

    self-made man, by himself,
    parked, under the parking lot lights.

VIII

Gull Sutra

When the front edge of a big westerly
stumbles in across the Coast Range, gulls
in the Willamette Valley get off the ground,
jump from parapets, drop from power poles
into the turbulent current. Temporarily
refraining from fishwife prattle, to focus,
they tack and tumble, wings unlocked,
taking most of the morning, if necessary,
to drift as much as a dozen miles east. Then,

when the day settles into a steady cold rain,
they swagger and poop with equanimity
on unfamiliar lawns, and squabble
with new pied rivals over a spilled sandwich
every bit as delectable on the deliquescent
pavement of the Safeway parking lot
in Stayton, as it might have been in Salem.

IX

*"… like a green girl,
   unsifted in such perilous circumstances"*

after the Klickitat raft capsized, they bobbed
along a while just fine, calling encouragement,
till right there, where the current curls over
that whale-shaped shelf, and Oksana got sucked
under and jammed in the narrow outlet
between the overhang and the heavy bottom
round rock where the killer vortex Venturi's
through, and, despite the life jacket, she couldn't
rise to the tempest surface for two dark days and
nights, whereupon she made a mermaid passage
to the Columbia, under the mid-summer sun
and winking alder shade, as a pack of bright jack
salmon flashed upstream, and a modest chorus
of meadowlarks sang of her beauty and courage

X

Unified Field Theory

At the high point of Territorial Road
just east of Tangent, Paul pulls over,
decants some citrus-flavored vodka
from a plastic pint in a paper bag
to an empty fast-food coffee cup,
takes a belt and a deep breath,
and watches as the winter sun
alights along the scrubby lea
beneath Pete's Mountain.
Our boy begins to grasp
that the world whirls,
and that every wort
across its curve
is realing
with
joy
.

XI

Robinson Creek

Skinny kid dislodges forty pound stone
from the Pleistocene conglomerate
where after centuries of tumbling to
become smooth and oblate like a Neolithic
nude it lay embedded in the gravel
stream a million years until that winter's
swollen creek exposed it to the grasp
of a sunburned child who dumps it as
the keystone into his rudimentary dam

Creek and kid, in kind, create
inconsequential disturbances that
are quickly erased and ultimately buried
but the pool is cool while it lasts and
the sculpted stone is shown briefly to the world

XII

minor enigma

a small enough carnage
can be hidden in the fold
of a single sheet of wax paper

but questions of ethics
remain: chuck it
into the garbage can
with other otherwise redeemable
bio waste, like
a wilted cabbage leaf?

or, more responsibly,
scrape it, naked,
with its little potent charge
of blood and bones and bile,
into the communal
compost pile?

XIII

Exercise no. 38

Pull your simple pickup
into a suitable spot
at the lower corner
of the big empty parking lot
of the new Walmart store
above McLoughlin Boulevard
at precisely 5:45 am, after
the forecast storm
has fully arrived from the coast;

kill the headlights,
shut it down, listen
to the idiot rain
tap dance on the roof of the cab

till your mind runs clear

XIV

Two Rivers

What the backhoe operator refers to as round rock,
and the mason calls aggregate, is actually
ancient gravel, burnished by the action of water
over a million years, buried in the silt of eroded
volcanic extrusions, and stripped raw by the river
to accommodate my sitting in its warmth, feet planted
in its cool grasp six inches deeper.
                                      A blood red rock
lies beside a blue rock, shot with a white line of mica.
Aside from varied minerality, they are precise copies,
lying in their billions in a bar a quarter mile long,
flowing imperceptibly, roughly parallel to the river,
to descend beneath the field where the fence tips
over the undermined blackberries, one post
bobbing in and out of the current like a drinking bird.

XV

Callus

Joe Meek dug the hole to bury Mary at the end
of a long day piling slash and burning stumps.
That morning, she had asked for his hand, and
he had given it, unfed and irritated, only hastily.
When, with God's help, and the sweatier variety
of Asahel Lambert, his Anabaptist neighbor,
they got her into the ground, he knelt a bit
and sought to meditate and fell, instead,
abruptly asleep. Stretched akimbo, Joseph lay,
while Lambert left, discreet amule, and there
he dreamed the night away, his aching back
against the spoils of funeral soil. Mary featured
largely, defying several buried children,
the burning barn, his anger … with dead kisses.

XVI

Deep Weed Theory

Gather your stomping to get through the weeds
as they rise to lift you halfway into fir wood;
this is the parcel behind the little war-time bungalows,
where the rednecks have failed to cause any trouble;
breach the blackberry and buckthorn far enough and
the view of Mt. Scott and Mt. Hood should be plain;
in between, if you pay attention, there is abundance
beneath each step, from foxglove through harebell
and pigweed to plantain upon warrens of coppery ants.
Why has it started to choke me up, of late,
to witness the world at almost any layer of sense?
Standing to my armpits in sword fern and fireweed,
I begin to twig that I am not, after all, any kind of
martyr; in transit, in fact, from heaven to Heaven.

XVII

weeds

sedge is solitary
an unlovely clump
of silvery rocket stems
arcing in stubborn celebration
of loneliness
dead middle
of the lately flooded muddy creek bar

further up the rubble ledge
indifferent cousin, rush,
sprouts in similar
disheveled dalliance

both ugly, in any case,
unless, as with many things,
you sit and watch a while

XVIII

Amaranthus viridis

Pigweed is not
the nephrite neon spark
of the arc between
the mineral third rail
of the A-train aquifer
rumbling in the gut
of the earth, electric,
and the sun digit
god-dangled from
the suddenly opening
spattered sash of the
rain tattered ion sky.

It is but pigweed,
and enough.

XIX

Hwy 99 North of Aurora

Under the bridge, the Pudding River chugs brown
between margins of neon green and the black mud
where winter cattle slog. A calico border collie steps
to the cow trough to drink urbanely of its black water.
Crossing the bridge in his basic truck, observing
the condition of the river and the demeanor of the dog,
the man hears Russian choral music on the radio
and sips whisky from a plastic pint in a paper bag.
Having spent the early hours at the hospital in Salem,
alone, he is headed for home, or what was home,
perhaps to nap, or paint a nude, in gold and umber,
or play the blues on the grand piano by the window
green with rain, to read, to write, take a long hot bath,
or simply to sit at the table with his head in his hands.

XX

Alcoholic

At the dump to chuck
a prodigious load of shit
my son pulls
from the duff
the truncated stump
of a bloody rhododendron
ripped most in half
on the truck hitch chain
of a harried Mexican gardener
to make space for
zinnias

Four years later, my prize
blocks the drive
with bloom

XXI

Bliss Road, west Benton County

braid the rain
lay its clean wet rope
among the rocks along the creek

haul down the clouds
onto the sprouted slopes
to let the land drink their big liquor

will the hills to dwindle
trees cease, blue sky evaporate
allow your tomfool truck to vanish

ditch the body. what remains?
a wave of transport, proceeding
from now to no particular where

XXII

Seeing Things

Osprey rises, laboring between two concrete road ramps,
freighted with a fish blitzed from the drainage ditch below.
this fish lacks a back, its oily dorsum eaten deeply crescent
… to lighten the load? but how? socked in the hawken crop,
the weight of bird and lately swimmer equal either way.

Mystery is busy in each layer of our witnessing:
like the light made by weeds in a long-dead snarl
charged with trash and faceted conflagration,
roadside as we race into a flood of darkening wind.

At any rate, the finned one takes now to the air,
talon-fast, face forward with finally drying eyes,
so the fishy death epiphany features a fading reconnaissance
of freeway and factories and the aural shush, not of water,
but of wings.

XXIII

unchosen

when, as so often,
a little germinant bird
gets ejected early,
it returns
its modest soul
to a waiting place
that rarely
opens its door
upon grass and water

not a room, though,
walls all gone

god's gaze
distant
as the winter sun

XXIV

regarding wife

twenty paintings
a hundred poems

five thousand sex tickets
punched, scattered on the wind

half a million minutes
gazing at her dimpled face

lovely Chinese girl
thoroughly witnessed

precautions against, her being
gone, there is no record

Acknowledgments

The author gratefully acknowledges previous publication of the following poems:

Sonnet recited in one long breath	*Turtle Island Quarterly*
Regarding Wife	*Big Bridge*
cover	*Juked*
warts across the flank of infinity	*Turtle Island Quarterly*
rehearsal	*The Lake*
mendicant	*Cider Press Review*
Gull Sutra	*Hamilton Stone Review*
" … like a green girl, unsifted …"	*Up The Staircase Quarterly*
Unified Field Theory	*Eunoia Review*
minor enigma	*Turtle Island Quarterly*
Exercise no. 38	*The Lake*
Two Rivers	*The Fourth River*
Callus	*West Coast Anthology*
Deep Weed Theory	*Centrifugal Eye*
amaranthus viridus	*Turtle Island Quarterly*
Hwy 99 North of Aurora	*Poetry Quarterly*
unchosen	*right hand pointing*

About the Author

A carpenter, Ted writes, paints, and plays tennis with lovely Amy Lee. Nominated twice for Best of the Net, and twice for the Pushcart Prize, his work appears in *Beloit Poetry Journal*, *[PANK]*, *DIAGRAM*, *Juked*, *Gargoyle*, *Magma*, and dozens of other publications.

www.ingramcontent.com/pod-product-compliance
Lightning Source LLC
Chambersburg PA
CBHW060804070426
42449CB00046B/3154